LIMERICKS FOR THE CONNOISSEUR

collected and edited by
Jeremy Nicholas

Published by New Generation Publishing in 2019

Copyright © Jeremy Nicholas 2019

First Edition

The author asserts the moral right under the Copyright, Designs and Patents Act 1988 to be identified as the author of this work.

All Rights reserved. No part of this publication may be reproduced, stored in a retrieval system or transmitted, in any form or by any means without the prior consent of the author, nor be otherwise circulated in any form of binding or cover other than that which it is published and without a similar condition being imposed on the subsequent purchaser.

www.newgeneration-publishing.com

 New Generation Publishing

For my fellow members

FOREWORD

The limerick packs laughs anatomical
Into space that is quite economical.
But the good ones I've seen
So seldom are clean
And the clean ones so seldom are comical.

No one has yet read the introduction to a book of limericks. At least, I've never met anyone who has. But I would ask you, dear potential customer, to read this bit before forking out your hard-earned dosh. If you are the kind of person who is offended by the lewd, the explicit, the politically incorrect and the liberal use of old Anglo-Saxon and Medieval swear words, then close this book now. Put it back on the shelf. Desist!

If you could be described as a snowflake or if you are one of that newly-evolved social media breed who take offence on behalf of someone else who they think might be offended by something done or said to them... then this little volume is not for you either. Don't be tempted by that Amazon 'Add to basket' button. Don't buy it - please! Really. Go and have a coffee. Put it out of your mind.

For the rest of you – welcome! Come on in!

Goodness knows how many books of limericks have been published over the years. My own library boasts a modest fifteen volumes of various shapes and sizes. What need of another? Well, most collections go for quantity rather than quality. This one goes for quality.

A high proportion of limericks in most collections do not meet the basic rules of the limerick form. Many do not scan or rhyme properly and seem to be there merely to fill out the page.

You see, there are several ineluctable laws that govern the construction of a successful limerick: it has to tell a complete story or make its point within the space of five lines; the rhyming pattern must be A-A-B-B-A; it must scan with the rhythmically-correct number of syllables – hymnologists would define the metre as 8 8. 5 5. 8; it must be grammatically correct; it must make you laugh, or at least make you smile by its ingenuity.

If it fails in any of these respects, the whole mechanism collapses – and I have been ruthless in excising (with few exceptions) any that do not fulfil all those requirements. To give you an example of the merciless approach I have taken in making my selection, I have omitted (albeit with some regret) Miss Myra MacLeod whose story has found its way into several collections:

> At shooting, Miss Myra MacLeod
> With exceptional gifts was endowed.
> But it wasn't her pistols
> So much as her Bristols [1]
> That Myra's admirers admired.

Admittedly, it has its good points (if you'll pardon the expression) but sadly, while 'MacLeod' and 'endowed' rhyme, neither of them rhyme with 'admired'.

Other limericks either make no grammatical sense or - the greatest sin of all - are simply dull.

For that reason, none of those by Edward Lear, frequently but mistakenly credited with the invention of the limerick (though he certainly popularised the form), have made the grade. His last lines are almost always a repeat of the first lines. That won't do at all these days: the last line is the pay-off, the punch line, the unexpected denouement of the five-line drama. Charming and sweet though Lear's limericks may be, they don't make you laugh by their subject matter or the cleverness of their rhyme.

---

[1] Rhyming slang: Bristol City = titty, though why Bristol and not, say, Leicester, is unclear.

Maligned and frowned upon in some quarters, a good limerick is a tricky thing to write.

> It's partly the shape of the thing
> That gives the old limerick wing.
> These accordion pleats
> Full of airy conceits
> Take it up like a kite on a string.

Almost all the limericks I have chosen have, at some time or other, been recited in front of an audience - at after-dinner speeches, during one of my one-man shows devoted to comic verse, in the pub, or at one of many riotous lunches at my club, to whose members this collection is dedicated. If they haven't got a laugh, they have not found their way into this volume.

Also, I have done some background research where appropriate. The observant will have noticed the little numeral after the word 'Bristols' (see above) used to describe Miss MacLeod's embonpoint. This indicates a footnote at the bottom of the page. Similarly, you might think that the place-name Baroda has simply been invented to provide a rhyme for 'soda'. Not so(da). You might think that the poet's mention of Mozart's Oboe Quartet in F major is spurious. Far from it. The footnote will quickly disabuse you. I have thrown in these and many others throughout the book – and at no extra charge.

Apart from this helpful resource, there is an index, so that it is but the work of a moment to look up that limerick about Lady Katrina Macduff or the one about the elephant's dong.

Old friends are here, mingled with newcomers and not a few strangers. All are by Anon. except for a small number where the author is known, identified in brackets at the end of the limerick. If I have failed to credit any writer, I sincerely apologise and will amend the omission in any future edition.

There are a number of quite well-known limericks which I have not included because, to me, they are either gratuitously crude or inelegant. Many are whiter than white, shining beacons of innocence for after all…

It needn't have ribaldry's taint
Or strive to make everyone faint.
There's a type that's demure
And perfectly pure -
Though it helps quite a lot if it ain't.
(*Don Marquis*)

Most, however, are either scatological, politically incorrect, offensive, tasteless or all five because – let's admit it – generally:

> The limerick's callous and crude,
> Its morals distressingly lewd.
> It's not worth the reading
> By persons of breeding –
> It's meant for us vulgar and rude.

That's me – and you, dear reader, who has now had the nous to read this introduction and is about to pay for this collection. Clearly you are a person of taste and discernment - and a connoisseur of this delightful verse form. I hope you enjoy it.

Jeremy Nicholas
Great Bardfield, 2018

On the breasts of a barmaid from Sale [1]
Was tattooed the price of pale ale.
On her big fat behind,
For the sake of the blind,
Was the same information in Braille.

Said the Duchess to me while at tea,
'Tell me, dear, do you fart when you pee?'
Replied I with some wit,
'Do you piss when you shit?'
Which I thought was one up to me.

There was a young fellow from Kent
Whose tool was exceedingly bent,
So to save himself trouble
He stuffed it in double -
And instead of coming, he went.

---

[1] A town in Cheshire

While Titian was mixing rose madder [1]
His model reclined on a ladder.
Her position to Titian
Suggested coition -
So he shinned up the ladder and had her.

There was a young lady from Coleshill [2]
Who sat by mistake on a mole's hill.
The resident mole
Stuck his nose up her hole.
Miss Coleshill's all right but the mole's ill.

There was a young man from St. Bees [3]
Who said to a girl on her knees,
'It would give me such bliss
If you took hold of this,
But be frightfully careful of these.'

---

[1] Titian (properly Tiziano Vecellio) c.1488-1576, the great Venetian painter. Madder is a plant whose root affords a red dye or other species of Rubia, part of the family of sympetalous dicotyledons akin to the *Caprifoliacae*. OK?

[2] A town in north Warwickshire about 20 minutes from the M6

[3] A smaller town near Egremont in Cumberland

There was young man from Nantucket [1]
Whose cock was so long he could suck it.
He said with a grin,
Wiping spunk from his chin,
'If my ear was a cunt, I could fuck it.'

There was a young curate from Crewe [2]
Who said, as the bishop withdrew,
'The vicar was slicker
And quicker and thicker
And three inches longer than you.'

OSSIA: There was a young lady from Kew
Who said, as the curate withdrew,
'I prefer the dear vicar -
He's longer and thicker.
Besides, he comes quicker than you.'

---

[1] On an island in the state of Massachusetts off the north east coast of America.

[2] Another town in Cheshire.

Also from Crewe...

There once was a cop from Crewe Junction
Who had sexually ceased to function.
For the rest of his life
He deceived his poor wife
With the dexterous use of his truncheon.

A lady while dining at Crewe
Found an elephant's dong in her stew.
Said the waiter, 'Don't shout
Or wave it about
Or the others will all want one too.'

There was a young lady of Crewe
Who wanted to catch the 2.02.
Said the porter, 'Don't worry
Or hurry or scurry,
It's a minute or two to 2.02.'

There was a young girl from Hong Kong
Who said, 'It is really quite wrong
To say my vagina's
The biggest in China
Because of your miserable prong.'

On the other hand...

There was a young girl from Detroit
Who at fucking was rather adroit.
She'd contract her vagina
To a pin-point or finer
Or flollop it out like a quoit.

And also...

A lovely young lady named Florrie
Bent over and fell in a quarry.
She lay on her back
And opened her crack
And a fella backed in with a lorry.

The same phenomenon can be observed on the Continent…

There was a young lady from Bruges
Whose cunt was enormous and huge.
Said Louis Quatorze [1]
As he pulled down her drawers:
'*Mon Dieu, après moi le déluge!*'

There was a young monk of Dundee
Who complained that it hurt him to pee.
He said, 'Pax vobiscum!
Now why won't the piss come?
I'm afraid I've the C-L-A-P.'

There was a young lady at sea
Who complained that it hurt her to pee.
'Aha!' said the mate,
'That accounts for the state
Of the cook and the captain and me.'

---

[1] Louis XIV known as Le Roi Soleil ('The Sun King') 1638-1715

A rare two-verse limerick:

A Sultan who lived in Algiers
Once said to his harem, 'My dears,
You may think it odd of me
But I've given up sodomy.
Tonight there'll be fucking.' (*Loud cheers*)

Up spake the Sultan's mahout [1]
Who said, 'But there isn't a doubt
That what really gives joy
Is a rosy-cheeked boy.'
(*Cries of 'Shame!', 'Filthy poof!', 'Chuck him out!'*)

Nymphomaniacal Alice
Used a dynamite stick as a phallus.
Her vagina was found
Thirty feet underground
And her arsehole in Buckingham Palace.

---

[1] The keeper and driver of an elephant.

Another young lady named Alice
Went and peed in a Catholic chalice.
It wasn't the need
That inspired the deed
But sheer Presbyterian malice.

To his bride, said a lynx-eyed detective,
'Can it be that my eyesight's defective?
Has your east tit the least bit
The best of the west tit
Or is it a trick of perspective?'

A surly and pessimist Druid -
A defeatist if only he knew it -
Said, 'The world's on the skids
And I think having kids
Is a waste of good seminal fluid.'

There once was a certain Miss Gale
Who turned most exceedingly pale,
For a mouse climbed her leg
(Don't repeat this, I beg)
And a splinter got caught in its tail.

A mathematician named Hall
Has a hexahedronical ball.[1]
And the cube of its weight
Times his pecker, plus eight,
Is his phone number. Give him a call!

A Scotsman called Robert the Bruce
Had a tartan of yellow and puce.
His friends asked 'Oh why does
He talk to those spiders?
D'ye think Bruce has got a screw loose?'
(*Jeremy Nicholas*)

---

[1] A hexahedron is a solid with six sides or faces

There was a young lady of Pecking [1]
Who indulged in a great deal of necking.
This seemed a great waste
Since she claimed to be chaste.
This statement, however, needs checking.

An agent of Walls in Manila
Found a market for sperm of gorilla.
He massaged their cocks
And then froze it in blocks
And sold it abroad as vanilla.

The Americas seems to breed salesmen with initiative…

A Chicago meat-packer named Young
One day, when his nerves were unstrung,
Pushed his wife's Ma - unseen -
In the chopping machine -
Then canned her and labelled her TONGUE.

---

[1] This must be poetic license. I cannot find anywhere that is called Pecking.

There was a young man from Porthcawl [1]
Who went to a fancy-dress ball.
He decided to risk it
And go as a biscuit
But a dog ate him up in the hall.

Said the Duchess of Alba to Goya, [2]
'Remember that I'm your employer!'
So he painted her twice –
Once clothed (which was nice)
And once in the nude to annoy her.

A Crusader's wife slipped from the garrison,
And had an affair with a Saracen;
She was not over-sexed,
Or jealous or vexed,
She just wanted to make a comparison.
(*Ogden Nash*)

---

[1] A town roughly midway between Cardiff and Swansea

[2] The 12th Duchess of Alba (1761-1802), or Doña Maria de Pilar Teresa Cayetana de Silva Álvarez de Toledo, was indeed painted both fully clothed and naked by her lover, the great Spanish painter Francisco de Goya (1746-1828) sometime between 1795 and 1800.

I sleep very well since we parted,
So really I'm not broken hearted.
I still think you're a prude
To say I was rude
To laugh at your Mum when she farted.

Said Wellington, 'What's the location
Of this battle I've won for the nation?'
They replied, 'Waterloo.'
He said, 'That'll do.
What a wonderful name for a station!'
(*Frank Richards*)

There was a young lady named Pager
Who, as the result of a wager,
Consented to fart
The whole oboe part
Of Mozart's Quartet in F major. [1]

---

[1] Composed c.1781, this is K370 in Köchel's catalogue of Mozart's works.

There was an upholsterer named Bryce
Who wasn't, quite honestly, nice.
He stuffed his armchairs
With the wee pubic hairs
That he plucked from the scrotums [1] of mice.

There once was a man from Baroda [2]
Who would *not* pay a whore what he owed her.
With great savoir faire
She stood on a chair
And pissed in his whisky and soda.

An ambitious young sculptor named Day
Once fashioned a cunt out of clay.
The heat from his prick
Baked the clay into brick
And scraped all his foreskin away.

---

[1] As a second declension neuter noun, the correct plural of scrotum is, of course, scrota. But it's not as funny.

[2] Town in India about 150 kms SSW of Jaipur.

An accident really uncanny
Occurred to my elderly Granny.
She sat in a chair
While her false teeth lay there
And bit herself right in the fanny.

There once was a poof from Newcastle
Who wrapped up a turd in a parcel.
He sent it by post
To a friend on the coast
To show him the size of his arsehole.

An elderly gasman named Peter,
While hunting around his gas heater,
Touched a leak with his light.
He rose out of sight –
And, as anyone who knows anything about
poetry can tell you, he also ruined the meter.

There was a young man from Herne Bay [1]
Who was making explosives one day,
But he dropped his cigar
In the gunpowder jar.
There was a young man from Herne Bay.

There once was a man tore his hide
To find out just what was inside.
He ripped and he tore
Till his hands ran with gore,
But before he could find out he died.

There was a young girl from the Cape
Who was fucked by a Barbary ape.
The outcome was 'orrid -
All bum and no fore'ead
And one of its balls was a grape.

---

[1] Or Hernia Bay as it is known to some because of the average age of its inhabitants. Pleasant seaside town on the Kent coast which had the second longest pier in the UK until 1978.

Have you heard of the Marquess of Bute [1]
Who buggered himself with a flute?
He'd enough room therein
For a whole violin -
The bow and the strings and the mute.

There was a young man from Calcutta [2]
Who was writing up *F U C K* on a shutter.
He had just reached *F U*
When a pious Hindu
Knocked him arse-over-tit in the gutter.

There was a young lady from Beaune [3]
Who didn't have one of her own.
She really felt sad
Till she saw *The Times* ad.:
'Rent-A-Twat - write, call or phone'.
(*Bill Hays*)

---

[1] A title in the peerage of Great Britain created in 1796 for John Stuart, 4th Earl of Bute.

[2] Reverted in 2001 to its original Bengali name of Kolkata. Unfortunately, it doesn't rhyme with 'shutter' or 'gutter'.

[3] The wine capital of Burgundy situated in the east of France.

And now, one of the truly great examples of the genre, and one that demands a commentary.

My dear Mrs. Featherstonehaugh, [1]
You really are rather a bore.
I'm covered in sweat
And you haven't come yet -
And look at the time! Half-past four!! [2]

---

[1] Pronounced 'Fan-shaw', of course. But not here.

[2] This apparently simple story begs many a question, its five lines furnishing enough material for a novella. We do not know the identity of Mrs Featherstonehaugh's lover but he is clearly well-educated, considerate and, from his manner of speech, most probably from the upper-classes. Who is this (obviously) married lady with whom he seems to be having an affair? How did they meet? How long have they been lovers? Where are they making love? How long have they been making love? We know from the evidence of the lover's watch – or maybe a bedside clock - that it is an afternoon tryst. Why has he become anxious about the time? Is Mr Featherstonehaugh due home at any minute? Might he disrupt the passionate love-making so unsatisfactorily in progress? Perhaps the lover is supposed to be somewhere else by five o'clock – maybe he has arranged to meet his wife at that time - but does not want to abandon his mistress until she has reached orgasm. He shows every sign of being a thoughtful and sensitive individual in this regard but, clearly, having put so much time and energy into his love-making, he is now becoming impatient for a conclusion. Whatever the mysterious circumstances may be, one rather fears for the long-term future of their relationship.

Count Palmiro Vicarion offers an alternative version in his seminal *Book of Limericks* (The Olympia Press, 1962)

'My back aches. My penis is sore.
I simply can't fuck any more.
I'm dripping with sweat,
And you haven't come yet:
And my God it's a quarter to four.'

A young violinist called June
Turned up for rehearsals too soon
And a man in the band
Put his flute in her hand
And it changed to a contra-bassoon.

Those two horrid men Foss and Goss
Once tried to put it across
A young girl in a train -
But their hopes were in vain,
So Goss tossed off Foss to King's Cross.

A volcanic eruption in Java
Afforded Lord Dufferin and Ava [1]
In a moment sublime
To record for all time
The imprint of his cock in some lava.

There was a young fellow named Hall
Who fell in the spring in the fall.
'T would have been a sad thing
Had he died in the spring,
But he didn't - he died in the fall.

A banker whose mistress had sighed
For a gift of some golf clubs she'd spied
Didn't hear his love mutter
'Two woods and a putter',
So he bought her St. Andrews and Ryde [2].

---

[1] Irish title. The first Marquess was Frederick Temple Hamilton-Temple-Blackwood (1826-1902).

[2] St. Andrews ('the home of golf') is situated on the northeast coast of Scotland, just south of Dundee. So the mistress would have a long journey from there to her other clubhouse, Ryde, on the Isle of Wight.

There was a young fellow named Carter
Who was quite a remarkable farter.
On the strength of one bean
He'd fart *God Save The Queen*
And Beethoven's 'Moonlight' Sonata. [1]

A young violinist from Rio
Was seducing a singer called Cleo.
As he took off her panties
She said, 'No *andantes* -
I want this *allegro con brio.*'

A Millwall supporter named Joe
Was attacked by five skinheads from Bow.
As he drew a last breath,
He intoned at his death
'Here we go, here we go, here we go.' [2]

---

[1] The popular name for Beethoven's piano sonata No. 14 in C♯ minor *'Quasi una fantasia'*, Op. 27 No. 2, composed in 1801. It has three movements, testament to Carter's phenomenal fartmanship.

[2] Traditional mindless football supporters' lyric, sung to the tune of 'The Star-Spangled Banner'.

There was a young man up at Trinity
Who first took his sister's virginity,
Then buggered his brother,
Had twins by his mother
And still got a first in divinity.

A vice both obscure and unsavoury
Held the Warden of Wadham [1] in slavery.
With lecherous howls
He buggered small owls
In a secret underground aviary.

There was a young lady from Bude [2]
Who danced on the stage in the nude,
When a bloke in the front
Shouted, 'Look at her cunt!'
Just like that. Right out loud. Bloody rude.

---

[1] Wadham College, Oxford has had a Warden since its foundation in 1610. I have been unable to discover to which of the many holders of this office the limerick refers.

[2] A lovely seaside resort in north Cornwall just off the A39.

There was a young fellow named Skinner
Who took a young lady to dinner.
At exactly half nine
They sat down to dine
And by quarter past ten it was in her.
What, dinner?
No, Skinner.

Another Skinner, perhaps the sister of the above, had an embarrassing experience as relayed in this coprophilous verse:

There was a young lady named Skinner
Who dreamt that her lover was in her.
She awoke with a start
And let out a loud fart,
Which was followed by luncheon and dinner.

There was a young lady named Jane
Who liked a fuck now and again.
Not now and again
As in 'now and again',
But 'Now! And again! And again!'
(*Leo McKern*)

A young lady from Henley-in-Arden [1]
Was down on her knees in the garden.
The chap said, 'Dear Flo,
Where does all that stuff go?'
And she said, '(*swallow hard*) – I beg pardon?'

There was a young man from Australia
Who painted his bum like a dahlia.
The drawing was fine,
The colour divine,
But the scent? Ah! The scent was a failure.

---

[1] Picturesque town in Warwickshire, not to be confused
with Henley-on-Thames about 75 miles south and where
they have the regatta.

A variant of this is:

There was a young man from Westphalia [1]
Who painted his arse like a dahlia.
At twopence a smell
It went every well,
But fourpence a lick was a failure.

There was a young man of Peru
Who was hard up for something to do,
So he took out his carrot
And buggered his parrot
And sent the results to the zoo.

There was a young lady of Rheims
Who, amazingly, pissed in four streams.
When a friend poked around,
A coat button was found
Wedged tightly in one of her seams.

---

[1] Region of north-west Germany.

There was a young plumber from Leigh [1]
Who was plumbing a girl by the sea.
Said the girl, 'Cease your plumbing,
There's somebody coming.'
Said the plumber, still plumbing, 'It's me.'

A young married couple named Kelly
Were found stuck belly to belly,
Because in their haste
They'd used library paste
Instead of petroleum jelly.

---

[1] It is unclear to which of the many towns bearing the name Leigh this refers, but the one in Dorset is nearer the coast than any other. Norman Douglas in his classic collection *Some Limericks* (Hutchinson & Poole, 1928) is convinced the plumbing is taking place in the Essex town of Leigh-on-Sea where he once lived. But 'It is not on the sea,' he avers. 'It is on the estuary of the Thames... Mudflats are to my eyes the chief beauty of Leigh. Picturesque, abundantly; but quite unfitted for plumbing purposes. Think of the girl's dress!'

This sort of unfortunate occurrence is not always accidental...

There was a young harlot from Kew
Who filled her vagina with glue.
She said with a grin
'If they pay to get in
They can pay to get out of it too.'

A young trapeze artist named Bracht
Is faced by a very sad fact:
Imagine his pain
When again and again
He catches his wife in the act.

There was a young man from Torbay [1]
Who set sail for China one day.
He was pinned to the tiller
By a sex-starved gorilla -
And China's a bloody long way.

---

[1] A borough in Devon, England, spanning the towns of Torquay, Paignton and Brixham. Not funny – but interesting.

A widow whose singular vice
Was to keep her late husband on ice,
Said, 'It's been hard since I lost him -
I'll never defrost him.
Cold comfort, but cheap at the price.'

There was a young girl from Darjeeling [1]
Who could strip-tease with exquisite feeling.
Not a murmur was heard,
Not a sound, not a word,
But the fly-buttons hitting the ceiling.

A daring young lady of Guam [2]
Observed, 'The Pacific's so calm
I'll swim out for a lark.'
She met a large shark ...
Let us now sing the 91st Psalm.

---

[1] Better known for its teas than strip-tease.

[2] The island is east of the Phillipines. Some may question
the choice of Psalm 91 in these sad circumstances. Verse 10
reads: 'Here shall no evil befall thee, neither shall any
plague come nigh thy dwelling.'

From the depths of the crypt at St. Giles
Came a scream that resounded for miles.
Said the vicar, 'Good gracious!
Has Father Ignatius
Forgotten the Bishop has piles?'

Rosalinda, a pretty young lass,
Had a truly magnificent ass:
Not rounded and pink
As you possibly think -
It was grey, had long ears and ate grass.

There was a young lady named Hilda
Who went driving one night with a builder.
He said that he should,
That he could and he would
And he did and it damn nearly killed her.

There once was a Bishop of Birmingham
Who seduced lots of girls while confirming 'em.
To rounds of applause
He would pull down their drawers
And pump the episcopal sperm in 'em.

When the Birmingham Water Board struck
The foreman was having a fuck.
But the union rules said
'Down with all tools'.
Now wasn't that jolly bad luck?

There was a young fellow named Hyde
Who fell down a toilet and died.
His unfortunate brother
Then fell down another
And now they're interred side by side.

There once was a clergyman's daughter
Who detested the pony he'd bought her
Till she found that its dong
Was as hard and as long
As the prayers that her father had taught her.

There was a young lady from Sydney
Who could take it right up to her kidney.
But a man from Quebec
Shoved it up to her neck.
He had a long one, now didn' he?

'It's true,' confessed Jane, Lady Norris. [1]
'I beg lifts from the drivers of lorries.
When they get out to piss
I see things that I miss
At the wheel of my two-seater Morris.'

---

[1] The Norris family is related to the Earls of Berkshire
(now incorporated with the titles of the Earl of Suffolk). I
rather like the sound of Lady Jane and her Girl Guide
sense of adventure.

Said a boy to his teacher one day,
'Wright has not written "rite" right, I say.'
And the teacher replied,
As the error she eyed,
'Right! Wright – write "rite" right, right away!'

There was a young gaucho named Bruno
Who said, 'Screwing is one thing I *do* know.
A woman is fine,
And a sheep is divine,
But a llama is *numero uno*.

There was a young lady of Exeter [1]
So pretty that men craned their necks at her.
One was even so brave
As to take out and wave
The distinguishing mark of his sex at her.

---

[1] Another Devon location. The city of Exeter boasts a beautiful Gothic cathedral. Well worth a visit if you haven't been.

There once was a dentist named Stone
Who saw all his patients alone.
In a fit of depravity
He filled the wrong cavity.
Gosh, how his practice has grown!

There was a young man of high station
Who was found by a pious relation
Making love in a ditch
To - I won't say a bitch -
But a woman of no reputation.

A wandering tribe called the Siouxs [1]
Wear moccasins, having no shiouxs.
They are made out of buckskin
With the fleshy side in,
Embroidered with beads of bright hyiouxs.

---

[1] The Siouxs were nomadic North Americans whose territory was in Minnesota, Wisconsin, and North and South Dakota. The name 'Sioux' means 'little snakes'.

Ethnologists up with the Sioux
Wired home for 'Two punts, one canoe.'
The answer next day
Said: 'Girls on the way,
But what in hell's name's a panoe?'

Pope John Paul II once spent
The weekend in Burton-on-Trent. [1]
He had beef, he had duck
And a barmaid to fuck -
But he couldn't because it was Lent.

There was a young fellow named Bliss
Whose sex life was strangely amiss.
For even with Venus
His recalcitrant penis
Would seldom do better than t
h
i
s.

---

[1] A town on the River Trent in East Staffordshire.

A maiden at college named Breeze,
Weighed down by B.A.s and Litt.D.s,
Collapsed from the strain.
Alas, it was plain
She was killing herself by degrees.

There once was a monk from Kintyre [1]
Who was seized with a carnal desire.
And the primary cause
Was the abbess's drawers
Which were hung up to dry by the fire.

A poofter who lived in Khartoum [2]
Took a lesbian up to his room,
And they argued all night
Over who had the right
To do what and with which and to whom.

---

[1] There was indeed a monastery on the east coast of the
Kintyre peninsula (Scotland). The Cistercian order
flourished in Saddell Abbey from 1148-1508.
[2] Capital and largest city of Sudan.

There was a young rector of King's [1]
Whose mind was on heavenly things,
But his heart was on fire
For a boy in the choir
With a bottom like jelly on springs.

A lady with features cherubic
Was famed for her area pubic.
When they asked her its size
She replied in surprise,
'Are you speaking of square feet or cubic?'

There was a young lady of Nantes [2] -
A girl *très jolie* et *piquante* -
But her cunt was so small
It was no good at all
Except for the *plume de ma tante*.

---

[1] Obviously King's College, Cambridge, founded in 1441
and famous for its Chapel – and choir.
[2] A town in western France located on the Loire.

Three bright little boys from the ballet
Had a lovely night out at the Palais,
But the end of their day,
I am sorry to say,
Was spent with three Burghers from Calais. [1]

In his bath mused the Marquis of Byng: [2]
'Ah, Vimy, what memories you bring!
That lovely young trooper...
I mean...Gladys Cooper! [3]
My goodness, that *was* a near thing!'

---

[1] What the six of them got up to that night is nobody's business but theirs. However, historically there were six Burghers of Calais, not three, if you remember your O Level or GCSE history. Rodin made a statue of them in 1889.

[2] Julian Hedworth George Byng (of Vimy), 1st Viscount (1862-1935), commander of the Canadian Army Corps at the capture of Vimy Ridge (1916-17).

[3] Dame Gladys Cooper (1888-1971), actress and one of the great beauties of the day.

There was a young man of Belgravia [1]
Who cared not for his God or his Saviour.
He walked down the Strand
With his balls in his hand
And was had for indecent behaviour.

Our vicar's an absolute duck -
But just now, he's down on his luck.
At the Sunday School treat
He tripped over his feet,
And all of us heard him say
'Now children, let us stand and say grace'.

On vacation last year in Bangkok, [2]
Imagine my panic and shock
As I gazed in her eyes,
Put my hand 'tween her thighs,
And instead of a cunt found a cock!
(*A. Steven*)

---

[1] Smart area of London close to Buckingham Palace. A decent sized town house will cost you between £25-30 million. One really would not expect anyone from Belgravia to expose their genitals in the Strand or anywhere else.

[2] The capital of Thailand which is in Asia, but without googling it I couldn't tell you exactly where.

Advertisement in a North American newspaper:

Evangelical vicar in want of a portable second-hand font would dispose of the same for a portrait (in frame) of the Bishop-Elect of Vermont.

There was a young farmer named Morse
Who fell madly in love with his horse.
Said his wife, 'You rapscallion -
That horse is a stallion!
This constitutes grounds for divorce.'

There's that notable family Stein :
There's Gertrude, there's Ep and there's Ein. [1]
Gert's prose is bunk,
Ep's sculpture is junk,
And no one can understand Ein.

---

[1] Gertrude Stein (1874-1946), writer, Jacob Epstein (1880-1959), sculptor, and Albert Einstein (1879-1955), theoretical physicist.

At last I've seduced the au pair
With some steak and a chocolate éclair,
Some peas and some chips,
Three Miracle Whips,
And a carafe of *vin ordinaire*.

There was a young poet of Kew
Who failed to emerge into view;
So he said, 'I'll dispense
With rhyme, metre and sense.'
And he did, and he's now in *Who's Who*.

There was a young lady from Tottenham-
Her manners, she'd totally forgotten 'em.
While at tea at the vicar's
She took off her knickers
Explaining she felt much too hot in 'em.

Prince Philip one day with his mucker
Went to Cowdray Park [1] for a chukka.
Said his friend: 'Your Royal High.,
Is the Queen passing by?'
He said: 'I don't know. Possibly. Fuck her.'
(Trevor Peacock)

In the Garden of Eden lay Adam
Complacently stroking his madam.
And loud was his mirth
For on all of the Earth
There were only two balls and he had 'em.

There was a young lady from Wick [2]
Who said to her Mum, 'What's a prick?'
She said, 'My dear Annie,
It goes up your fanny
And jumps up and down till it's sick.'

---

[1] Cowdray Park in West Sussex is home to the Cowdray Park Polo Club, one of the leading polo clubs in the United Kingdom. The sport has been played here for over 100 years.
[2] Wick is a Royal Burgh in the north of Scotland.

Happy-go-lucky Miss Hopper
Likes to be shagged good and proper -
Which is all very fine,
But she screws all the time
And I've blisters all over my chopper.

The wife of the Bishop of Mimms [1]
Was possessed of an outsize in quims.
But the Dean of the diocese
Had elephantiasis -
So life wasn't all singing hymns.

A Scots poet named Alan McNamiter
Had a tool of prodigious diameter.
Yet it wasn't the size
Gave the girls a surprise,
But his rhythm - iambic pentameter.

---

[1] A misnomer by the author. The parish of South Mimms, north of London and including the village of Potter's Bar, is actually a perpetual curacy in the gift of the Bishop of London.

Oh sexy, salacious Miss Plum!
When I asked her which way she had come,
She answered, 'By train.'
I replied, 'Come again?'
And she did, several times, on my thumb.

Young folk who frequent picture palaces
Have no need of psycho-analysis,
But I think Dr. Freud
Would be rather annoyed
That they cling to their long-standing fallacies.

An aspiring young lawyer named Rex
Was sadly deficient in sex.
Arraigned for exposure,
He replied with composure:
'De minimis non curat lex'. [1]

---

[1] 'The law does not concern itself with small matters'

A mosquito was heard to complain
That the chemists had poisoned his brain.
The cause of his sorrow
Was Paradichloro-
trimethyldichloroethane.[1]

There was a young artist named Saint
Who swallowed some samples of paint.
All shades of the spectrum
Flowed out of his rectum
With a colourful lack of restraint.

From Number 9, Penwiper Mews[2]
There is really abominable news:
They've discovered a head
In the bin for the bread,
But nobody seems to know whose.
(*attributed to Edward Gorey*)

---

[1] Molecular formula: $ClCH_2CH_2Cl$, better known as ethylene dichloride (EDC). So there.

[2] This compelling story, surely worthy of Agatha Christie, has in fact inspired a brief novella with that title. It seems to be about vampires, so I couldn't be bothered to buy a copy.

To a daughter, just married in Bicester, [1]
Her mother said (just as she kissed her)
'I say, you're in luck –
He's a jolly good fuck.
I know it – and so does your sister.'

A man in a bus queue at Stoke [2]
Unzipped all his flies for a joke.
An old man gave a shout
And nearly passed out,
And a lady close by had a stroke.

An old archaeologist, Throstle,
Discovered a marvellous fossil.
He knew from the bend
And the knob on the end
'Twas the peter of Paul the Apostle.

---

[1] Pretty market town in N E Oxfordshire just of the M40 (Junction 9 if you're interested).
[2] Short for Stoke-on-Trent. It's quite near Burton-on-Trent (see the limerick about Pope John Paul 11). Must be something in the water.

'Nurse Sunshine of Bedfordshire weds'
Ran the headline I saw here at Fred's.
And the young lady's name
Was Miss Rosemary Frame.
On the ward she is sweet "Rose of Beds".
(*Jeremy Nicholas*)

He made such a hullaballoo
At finding no roll in the loo
That his mother said, 'Ted,
You've a tongue in your head!'
'Ma, I'm not a giraffe in the zoo.'

A tutor who tooted the flute
Tried to tutor two tooters to toot.
Said the two to the tutor
'Is it harder to toot or
To tutor two tooters to toot?'

A girl who weighed many an ounce
Used language I dare not pronounce,
For a fellow unkind
Pulled her chair out behind
Just to see (so he said) if she'd bounce.

A sad poetess was young Jenny.
Her limericks weren't worth a penny.
In technique they were sound
But, however, she found
That whenever she tried to write any
She always wrote one line too many

There was a young man from Japan
Whose limericks never would scan
When someone asked why
He replied with a sigh
'It's because I always try to get as many words in
the last line as I possibly can.'

Another young poet in China
Had a feeling for rhythm much finer.
But his limericks tend
To come to an end
Quite suddenly.

Lady Katrina MacDuff [1]
Has a lovely luxuriant muff.
A golfer she knew
While trying to screw
Lost both of his balls in the rough.

There was a young woman called Gloria
Who was had by Sir Gerald du Maurier, [2]
By six other men,
Sir Gerald again,
And the band of the Waldorf Astoria. [3]

---

[1] Perhaps a descendant of Macbeth's antagonist.

[2] Sir Gerald Hubert Edward Busson du Maurier (1873 – 1934) was an English actor and manager, and father of the novelist Daphne du Maurier

[3] I am reliably informed that the original of this was 'the Brixton Astoria', a huge theatre in the south London suburb built in 1929.

Today's cinematic emporium
Is not just a visual sensorium
But a highly effectual
Heterosexual
Mutual masturbatorium.

An astronomer slept in the sun,
Then woke with his fly quite undone.
He remarked with a smile,
'Hoorah! A sundial!
And the time is a quarter past one.'

A notorious hooker named Hurst
In the weakness of men is well versed.
Reads a sign at the head
Of her often-used bed:
THE CUSTOMER ALWAYS COMES FIRST.

A worried young lad lived in Poole [1]
And discovered red marks on his tool.
Said the doctor, a cynic,
'Get out of my clinic
And wipe off the lipstick, you fool!'

'At a séance,' said a fellow named Post,
'I was being sucked off by a ghost.
Someone switched on the lights
And there, in silk tights
On his knees was old Basil, mine host.'

A pretty young maid from Peru
Had nothing whatever to do,
So she sat on the stairs
And counted cunt hairs –
5,602.

---

[1] Attractive costal town in Dorset.

'It has been a most excellent day,'
Yawned Lady McDougal McKay.
'Three cherry tarts,
At least twenty farts,
Two shits and a bloody good lay.'

That naughty old Sappho from Greece [1]
Said, 'What makes me feel really at peace
Is to have my pudenda
Rubbed hard by the enda
The snub little nose of my niece.'

There was a young man of Devizes [2]
Whose balls were of different sizes.
The left one was small –
Almost no ball at all –
But the other was big and won prizes.

---

[1] The author is clearly deeply versed in the Classics. Sappho was a Greek lyric poet (c.630 BC – c.570 BC). She was born on the island of Lesbos.

[2] Market town in Wiltshire.

There once was a tart from Marseilles
Who douched with a new type of spray.
Said she, 'Ah, that's better!
I've found that French letter
That's been missing since Armistice Day.'

There was a young lady from Ealing [1]
Who claimed to have no sexual feeling
Till a cynic named Boris
Just touched her clit*or*is [2]
And she had to be scraped off the ceiling.

A price-conscious hooker called Annie
Had a tariff both fair and quite canny:
A pound for a fuck,
Fifty pence for a suck
And two bob for a feel of her fanny.

---

[1] Third largest London Borough.

[2] One has to cheat slightly to make 'Boris' rhyme with 'clitoris'. Emphasise the second syllable.

Another two-verser returns us once more to the great city at the heart of the Midlands – and to the sexual proclivities of its clergy:

There once were two ladies from Birmingham.
Now here is a story concerning 'em.
They lifted the frock
And tickled the cock
Of the Bishop engaged in confirming 'em.

Now the Bishop was nobody's fool.
He'd been to a good public school,
So he pulled down his britches
And saw to those bitches
With his ten-inch episcopal tool.

There were three old ladies from Grimsby, [1]
Who wondered what for could their quims be.
They knew they could piddle
Through the holes in the middle,
But for what could the hairs round the rims be?

There was a young lady named Maxie
Who fancied a shag in a taxi,
But the bloke was so dim
That he quite missed her quim
And instead shoved it right up her jacksie.

The captain and crew are the best
And the sea air is giving me zest!
I am having, dear wife,
The time of my life
On this fine ship, the Marie Celeste...[2]
(*attrib. to Paul Chapman*)

---

[1] A large coastal English town in north-east Lincolnshire.
People from Grimsby are called Grimbarians or,
sometimes, Codheads.
[2] An American merchant brigantine, discovered adrift and
deserted in the Atlantic Ocean, off the Azores Islands, on
December 5, 1872

There was a young sailor named Bates
Who danced the fandango on skates.
He fell on his cutlass
Which rendered him nutless
And practically useless on dates.

There was a young lady of Trent [1]
Who said that she knew what it meant
When he asked her to dine –
Private room, lots of wine –
She knew, oh she knew! – but she went!

King Richard, in one of his rages,
Forsook his good lady for ages.
He rested in bed
With a good book instead,
Or, preferably, one of the pages.
(A.B. Hall)

---

[1] Trent is a town in Dorset, nothing to do with Burton-on
or Stoke-on.

There was a young curate of Kew
Who kept a tom-cat in a pew.
He taught it to speak
Alphabetical Greek
But it never got further than mew.

An undergrad up at St John's [1]
Attempted to bugger the swans,
But the kindly old porter
Said, 'Please take my daughter.
Them birds is reserved for the dons.'

An opera star from New York
Sang *Aida* [2] made up with burnt cork.
By way of an answer
A black ballet dancer
Did *Swan Lake* [3] just smothered with chalk.

---

[1] St John's, Cambridge or St John's, Oxford? My bet is the former – nearer the river and thus nearer the swans.
[2] Opera by Giuseppe Verdi and Antonio Ghislanzoni, first performed in 1871 to celebrate the opening of the new opera house in Cairo.
[3] Ballet by Tchaikovsky premiered in 1876.

On a maiden a man once begat
Bouncing triplets named Nat, Tat and Pat.
'Twas fun in the breeding
But hell in the feeding:
She hadn't a spare tit for Tat.

A bottle of perfume from Willie
Was highly displeasing to Millie.
Her response was so cold
That they quarrelled, I'm told,
Through that silly scent Willie sent Millicent.

An old Buddhist joiner from Ware [1]
Liked buttocks inviting and bare.
As some compensation
At his reincarnation
He returned as a cane-bottomed chair.

---

[1] Ware is in Hertfordshire near the county town of
Hertford. That's where Ware is.

A bankrupt young man from Geneva [1]
Fell asleep by the banks of the Weaver.
He awoke with a shock
To discover his cock
In the hands of the Official Receiver.

Concerning the Queen of Bulgaria, [2]
Her pudenda grew hairier and hairier.
The wretched old King
When he wanted a fling
Had to hunt for her cunt with a terrier.

---

[1] A sad tale (and one that has a last line which, strictly speaking, does not quite scan). The River Weaver rises between Chester and Northwhich, England. How a young Swiss fellow came to be in this part of the world without means of supporting himself must remain a mystery. And what was the Official Receiver – a civil servant when all's said and done - doing there during office hours?

[2] The Bulgarian royal family is a line of the Koháry branch of the House of Saxe-Coburg-Gotha which ruled Bulgaria from 1887 to 1946.

There once was a nun from Sofia [1]
Who succumbed to the abbot's desire.
She said, 'It's a sin,
But now that it's in
Could you shove it a few inches higher?'

A man with venereal fear
Had intercourse in his wife's ear.
She said, 'I don't mind,
Except that I find
When the telephone rings, I don't hear.'

And to end, an old favourite:

There was a young girl of Pitlochry [2]
Who was had by a man in a rockery.
She said, 'Oh! You've come
All over my bum!
This isn't a fuck. It's a mockery!'

---

[1] Sofia is the capital of Bulgaria.

[2] Beautiful little town slap in the middle of Scotland with a renowned Festival Theatre and a couple of nearby distilleries.

INDEX

Activity, Sexual 1-58 *passim*
        Aural 3, 58
        Fellatio 2, 24, 49, 51
        Incest 21
        Micturition 1, 6, 8, 14, 24, 32
        Necrophilia 28
        Up a ladder 1
        Up the Khyber 3, 7, 16, 22, 25, 29, 57
        With animals 15, 27, 30, 38, 57
        With birds 22, 25, 57
        With a dynamite stick 7
        With a flute 16
        With a truncheon 4
Aristocracy –
        Bulgaria, Queen of 57
        Bute, Marquess of 16
        Byng, Marquis of 36
        Duchess (unnamed) 1
        Dufferin and Ava, Lord 19
        Edinburgh, HM Duke of, (Prince Philip) 40
        Elizabeth 11, HM Queen 40
        Louis XIV, King 6
        MacDuff, Lady Katrina 47
        McKay, Lady McDougal 50
        Morris, Lady Jane 30
        Richard, HRH King 54
        Robert the Bruce, King 9
Arse (aka behind, bottom, bum, buttocks, jacksie, rectum) 1, 15, 24, 25, 36, 45, 55, 58, 60
Art & Artists 1, 11, 24, 25, 45
Breasts (aka Bristols, tits) iii, 1, 8, 58, 59
Clergy -
        Bishops (various) 3, 28, 29, 38, 41, 52
        Curates (various) 3, 4, 55
        Father Ignatius 28
        Miscellaneous 6, 31, 35, 36, 43
        Pope John Paul 33
        St Paul 44
        Vicars (various) 3, 4, 29, 39, 40, 41

Druid 8
Famous names –
        Adam 40
        Alba, Duchess of 11
        Beethoven, Ludwig van 20
        Braille, Louis 1
        Cooper, Dame Gladys 36
        Du Maurier, Sir Gerald 47
        Einstein, Albert 38
        Epstein, Jacob 38
        Freud, Dr Sigmund 42
        Goya, Francesco de 11
        Mozart, Wolfgang Amadeus 12
        Stein, Gertrude 38
        Titian 2
        Wellington, Duke of 12
Fart(ing) 1, 12, 12, 20, 22, 50
Fly-buttons 27, 46, 50
Gorilla 10, 26
Hairs, pubic 13, 35, 491, 53, 57
Ladies names -
        Alice (Nymphomaniacal) 7
           (Presbyterian) 8
        Breeze, Miss 34
        Cleo 20
        Featherstonehaugh, Mrs 17
        Florrie 5
        Gale, Miss 9
        Gloria, 47
        Hilda 28
        Hopper, Miss 41
        Jane, 23
        June 18
        MacLeod, Miss Myra, iii
        Maxie 53
        Plum, Miss 42
Music & Musicians 13, 15, 18, 20, 45, 47, 55
Paradichlorotrimethyldichloroethane 43
Penis (aka carrot, dong, tool, distinguishing mark, prong, carrot, phallus, pecker, chopper, prick, knob, peter), 1, 3, 4, 5, 9, 14, 19, 20, 25, 30, 31, 33, 35, 39, 42, 43, 51, 54

Bent 1
Definition of 40
Diameter 41
Elephant's 4
Fossilised 44
Frozen 27
Gorilla's 10
Imprint of 19
Injured 14, 41
Length 3, 5, 29, 52
Pony's 30
Recalcitrant 33
Red marks on 49
Sore 18

Place names -
Algiers 7
Bangkok 37
Bruges 6
Bulgaria 57
China 5, 26, 47
France
    Beaune 16
    Calais 36
    Marseilles 51
    Nantes 35
    Rheims 24
    Vimy 36
Geneva 57
Great Britain
    Bedforshire 45
    Belgravia 37
    Bicester 44
    Birmingham 29, 52
    Bow 20
    Buckingham Palace 7
    Bude 21
    Burton-on-Trent 33
    Coleshill 2
    Coiwdray Park 40
    Crewe 3, 4
    Devizes 50

Dundee 6
Ealing 51
Exeter 31
Grimsby 53
Henley-in-Arden 23
Herne Bay 15
Kent 1
Kew 3, 26, 39, 55
Kyntyre 33
Leigh (Dorset?) 25
Millwall 20
Newcastle 14
Pitlochry 58
Poole 49
Porthcawl 11
Ryde 19
St. Andrews 20
St. Bees 3
Scotland, 10, 18
Stoke (-on-Trent) 44
Trent 54
Torbay 26
Tottenham 39
Ware 56
Waterloo Station 12
Greece 50
Guam (island) 27
Hong Kong 5
India
Baroda 13
Calcutta 16
Darjeeling 27
Indonesia, 10
Japan 46
Khartoum 34
Manila 10
Peru 24, 49
Quebec 30
Rio de Janeiro 20
Sofia 58
Sydney 30

United States of America
    Chicago 10
    Detroit 5
Nantucket 3
Westphalia 24
Wick 40
Poets China, from 47
    Japan, from 46
    Jenny 46
    Kew, from 39
    MacNamiter, Alan 41
    Sappho 50
Psalm 91 27
Saracen 11
Sioux (Native Americans) 33
Strip-tease 27
Testicles (aka balls, scrota) 3, 9, 12, 15, 36, 40, 47, 50
    Care with 3
    Different shapes and sizes of 9, 25, 50
    Loss of 47
    Mice's 13
University college (various) 22, 35, 36, 57
Vagina (aka crack, cunt, fanny, hole, pudenda, quim, twat) 3, 5, 6, 7, 14, 17, 22, 27, 37, 39, 51, 55, 57
    Clay model of 13
    Filled with glue 26
    Size of 5, 6, 20, 35, 41
    Uncovered 21, 34, 47, 49, 55
Walls (ice-cream manufacturers) 10
Weaver, River 57

64

JEREMY NICHOLAS is an Olivier-nominated actor, award-winning broadcaster, writer and musician. President of the Jerome K Jerome Society and Director of Music for the archiepiscopal peculiar of St Mary's, Bocking, he lives in rural Essex with his first wife and a small dog.

For more information visit:
www.jeremynicholas.com

Lightning Source UK Ltd.
Milton Keynes UK
UKHW011840281220
376048UK00001B/90